Arthur Talks

Palewell Press

Arthur Talks

Poems by Ruth Hobson

Arthur Talks

First edition 2019 from Palewell Press,
www.palewellpress.co.uk

Printed and bound in the UK

ISBN 978-1-911587-23-1

All Rights Reserved. Copyright © 2019. No part of this publication may be reproduced or transmitted in any form or by any means, without permission in writing from the author. The right of Ruth Hobson to be identified as the author of this work has been asserted by her in accordance with the Copyright, Designs and Patents Act 1988

The cover design is Copyright © 2019 Camilla Reeve
The front cover photo is Copyright © 2019 BOULENGER Xavier / Shutterstock.com
The photo of Ruth Hobson is Copyright © 2019 Pavla Alchin

A CIP catalogue record for this title is available from the British Library.

Acknowledgements

A number of the poems first appeared in *Making Nothing Happen – Five Poets Explore Faith and Spirituality: D'Costa, Nesbitt, Pryce, Shelton and Slee*, Ashgate 2014.

'I asked a Man for a Light' was broadcast on the BBC's Morning Service programme in June 2005

'Remembering Earl' and 'When Pigeons Fall' were commended as runners-up in the Manchester Cathedral Religious Poetry Prize in 2011 and 2012 respectively.

Grateful thanks are also due to *Magma*, *The Delinquent*, and *Theology* journal, in which some of these poems first appeared.

Dedication

For all who have passed through the doors of
Emmanuel House Support Centre, Nottingham,
past and present, with respect.

Contents

I Asked a Man for a Light	2
After the Debacle	3
Bread	4
Hode Hidden	5
Arthur Talks	6
A One-Man Band Goes to Mass	7
Transport	8
Guinevere	9
Bravest	10
Book of Condolences	11
The Soundtrack	12
Brazier	13
Dog	14
Merlin Listens 1	15
Harp	16
Verbatim	17
When Pigeons Fall	18
Remembering Earl	19
In The Mandarin	20
Hymnody	21
Skip	22
The Sword in the Stone	23
Lost Reel	24
Merlin Listens 11	25
Round	26

Gallagher's Way	28
Circumstellar	30
Pianola	31
'There Will Be No More Temples in the City'	32
Gawain's Overcoat	34
Swedenborg's Drains	36
The Wedding Horse	37
The Craic	38
You Don't Have to Say Anything	39
Playing House	40
Arch	41
A Merry Christmas to all our Customers	42
The Turkey Who Lived on the Hill	44
The Order of Brightness	46
The End	47
Biography - Ruth Hobson	48

'There is another world and it's this one'
Attrib. Paul Eluard, Oeuvres completes,
Galliamard, Paris, 1968

'To live is to break
One's heart for the sake of love…'
Ueda Miyojh

I Asked a Man for a Light

I asked a man for a light, once,
and he gave it to me. Car lights
swam in the rain; cars hooted,
the bricks of the Night Shelter
red, black, wet, red, black,
blue, as clubbers parted around us.
I have this one rule, I call none of them
Sir. This one's face
bending towards me, was ordinary,
darkish, he'd cut himself shaving,
circles under his eyes.
It wasn't a great moment for me
I try to avoid this sort of thing,
and for him it would be forgotten
before it was over. If it were not
that he looked tired, and his lighter
was square and polished,
dark hairs on his thumb,
rain on his lapel,
and that, briefly, in the flame,
he looked at me,
I would have forgotten it myself.

After the Debacle

After the debacle, they gave me another key worker,
'Call me Rachel' I count her freckles, as she puzzles over
Assessment PD4 (to be filled in by the client)
'Now, Arthur,' 'I prefer to be called Mr. Rex.'

'Is it true that you have a tattoo on your left shoulder?'
Ah, the tattoos. Is it true? Is it true that this tattoo
was drawn with silver instruments? That, deep in the forest, maidens held
me down while a masked artist drew designs in the air with fire?

This pen's not working. For three days I lay
between death and life as they worked, and is it true,
(please use uppercase) that my whole body is a citadel, with a moat,
battlements and a great portcullis, a fortified town

that will never be breached, and certainly not by you, my dear.
'You lost your teeth during the incident? Well, Arthur,
here's the good news – they'll pay for a whole new set.'
A fortification, in fact, of incomparable beauty, gleaming in the sun.

Bread

A quantum of T. aestivum
indistinguishable among massed stars, turns
towards us, pulling around crashed moons,
becoming, as it comes, an atom of wheat,
a *genus*. Ears shiver, brushed by a rare light,
receiving cries, pleas, names; the seed falls,
interrupted by competing winds,
thrown off course but flowering, a harvest
heading for home.

Elroy, busking as usual, by Brixton nderground,
raises an eyebrow as a loaf of bread crash-lands
on the warm pavement. He keeps on singing,
watching the fragments break upwards, 783
then a 1000 more, straight into the cupped hands
of Isaac, sitting cross legged in his doorway,
straight into the open mouth of Lesedi,
aged 12, walking alone from Calais to
God knows where.

Hode Hidden

among leaves, cobnut brown on untrodden loam,
worsteds darkening with winter, then, like the magic hare,
mere movement in the snow. Against a tree, he's a tree

among many trees, endless, leaping from lit patch
to lit pool, never lost. His arrow speaks through the air,
birds, branches, the open road, chimes from the City,

toppling fruit, fanning fires, accompanying the demo
'No buts, stop the cuts', just missing the Castle's tourist map
'You are here'. Foxy notes the arrow without surprise,

the sign above his pitch says 'No Hoods Allowed'.
In the arrow's wake proffered notes ruffle,
heads turn, disconcerted. Share prices flutter,

shops and markets close, the streets empty.
Last seen astray in the runnels round Threadneedle Street,
never meeting its mark.

Arthur Talks

All you pools of dark around lamp-posts, you reflections in puddles,
you initials scratched in bus shelters, you sudden movements in skips
you lost macaws on flyers, you abandoned braziers,
you, Francine, from the telephone booth

listen

this is another story from The World's End All Nite Kaff,
where pictures of forgotten stars cut from newspapers
slip in their frames, and where on alternate Thursdays
leftover Cheesits are free.

'Morning, Arthur'

I sit at my table. They will bring me all I need,
Silver, napery, last week's Racing Post, a knowing look,
baked beans with extra toast. All is as ever.
Shake-a-Heart failed to run.

She's come.

A long shot to the far side of The World's End, the lashes,
the squashed-down beret, the light straight hair.
Grappling for the edge of the missing table-
where are my lines?

my sword?

The flicker fusion ratio adjusts. Close- up,
my ringed hand on hers. I open my mouth
and then she says
'Gimme a whisky, ginger on ze side, an' don't be stingee babee.'

A One-Man Band Goes to Mass

He pushes and doors open; boarded-up doors swing,
studded doors creak,
triangles of light fall on the pavements, the brick terraces.
Quick dip in the font,
notes flutter to the rafters, perch on the ledges.
Left and right his elbows plead
'I'm looking for a place, looking for a place'
and when two people part, to let him in,
the low note from the depths of his hat beeps twice.

Kneel down, One Man-Band, you've walked all day,
your home is this floor, carved with names,
beloved, not forgotten, rest in peace.
Names speak as you kneel, semi-quavers jump,
you bend your head;
a minor chord parts at the crossroads outside,
the traffic slows. I confess.
The drum on my back weighs heavy,
the drums on my ankles leaden, Amen.

Alleluia. The lost sheep on the hillside waits,
cymbals shivering; we hold our breath
as the shepherd climbs, listening for the airborne plea.
The horn sounds. Alleluia. I believe in the sound I make,
the echo from the crowds, the syncopation of feet
on the street. Now only the tinny rustle of listening;
you kneel like a bell, look up like a drum skin.
Bread lifts on the air with a crash, crumbs
fly to the door, doors open.

Transport

Late one afternoon, on the Piccadilly line
between Knightsbridge and Acton, where once
I'm told the Jarrow hunger marchers sat
in a terraced street, and the women ran out with food,
and a man with an eye-patch sitting next to me
said suddenly, very loudly
'Tierra del Fuego! Tierra del Fuego!'
A woman in a knitted beret with a thistle hatpin
was reading a typed manuscript, open on her knee,
'Wild Plants of the London Underground'
with each shudder of the train she mouthed
'Squirrel-tail Fescue, Fool's Watercress,
Mouse-Ear Hawkweed, Yarrow, Yarrow
and the train shook over a narrow bridge
and I saw a row of houses with yellow doors
and a woman taking pyjamas, sheets, towels, off the line
and when the person on the other side of me got off
at Barons' Court they left behind a half-open bag
and a clown costume was spilling out,
a red nose on elastic and some shiny cloth
with pompoms. I picked it up
with some idea of doing something – what?
and I wondered if someone had been a clown
and changed their mind, there and then,
wanting to be someone else, and was at that moment,
sitting on one of those wooden benches on the platform
with the station name along the back on enamelled metal panels-
one of many unique features of the London Underground.

Guinevere

She starts; a shape in the wind-blown dust
the name of my abiding lust.

The O of a skirt in an empty skip
bids my dreams unzip

then run, run to catch her train
a snatch of red in endless rain.

My love, my laughing one, my dear
who flies on the breath of every leer

who stands, aflood with neon yellow
proud gaze on the other fellow

pulling up his car. I know you well, my lover-queen,
your other name is 'might-have-been.'

Bravest

On the streets by 8 a.m.,
ready wigged and raising the alarm.
Steam spirals from gratings
beneath a wanted man, or two

on flapping posters. The daily tour begins,
plate glass offers her to him. He speaks
to small worlds, the cardboard rooms,
the sets of pans, lipstick like scarlet soldiers,

telling everything there is to know
about Princess Grace. Lamp posts listen to the tales
of the maharaja's pearls, the specially woven cashmere.
Her breasts swell in the telling.

Once he sported a mongrel, held on its string
like a jewelled poodle. Whether to have the sherbet
in pink and yellow layers, or jelly snakes
or a quarter of lime and chocolate éclairs?

She never buys, warmed by the sweet shop's
glamorous fires for another hour or so
Pulled from within, her attention
is spun, web-thin and trembling

from 8 a.m. to 8 p.m., when they let her back in.
Leon/Leonie, queen of the lonely
and boulevardier. Every day is double;
both rapture and trouble.

Book of Condolences

Aloysius, you were a gentleman, can't put my name.
Good luck mate, you was all right - The Boys.
With sympathy, Trace and all at the Phoenix Rd. Resettlement Team.
Mr. W. Birkenshaw. (Curly)
What's the Guinness like up there? Have one for me, Moz.
'This day you will be with me in Paradise'
'You were grand on the spoons' Blind Mary. Rest in Peace, Lou,
Addiction Services Room A. RIP Al,
You'll be missed, Lola B and all at the Dog and Partridge.

The Soundtrack

Pigeon named Voice
Pigeon named Source
Pigeon named Accordion
Pigeon named Sword-in Hand
Pigeon named Wanted
Pigeon named Hunted
Pigeon named Tattoo
Pigeon named Be True
Pigeon named Police at the Door
Pigeon named Grief Goes Before
Pigeon named Roll-Up
Pigeon named Foul-up
Pigeon named Brawl
Pigeon named Howl
Pigeon named Noble
Pigeon named Nobble
Pigeon named Sound
Pigeon named Beyond
Pigeon named *Exultate*
Pigeon named Party, Party!

Brazier

Only the frost spoke my name
graffiti on the black air
outside the halo of flames.
Other forms crouched by the warmth,
unfamiliar as speech.

Dog

divines the route, cheerfully
treading on cracks, under ladders,
heading straight for the cemetery,

shivering like a flame on the tombs,
rooting at the hems of angels,
warming selected inscriptions

with a blind paw. They all point
to heaven, but we keep going, crossing
the gallows site,

where a felon, refusing
his last pint, arrived on time
for execution, and missed his pardon.

More dangerous is your front door,
the visor which devoured
my letter, unreturned

like a fake Excalibur. Next,
the pub where I waited, left
and then you came,

past posters of gigs
we never went to. Turning the corner,
the smell-rope tugs him home,

like the lilies-of-the-field, he knows
he will be fed. A misunderstanding,
you said. There's nothing

that is not given. Further on,
look, the year's last conkers falling
on the graves of children.

Merlin Listens 1

Yeah, I asked and she goes yeah, it is.
This BLT's too salty.
It's the 10.33. Shit, I ain't got a watch.
You got a watch?
You sit here love, it's cold.
Do you know I've been trying claim my money back?
Visiting's from 11.30-3.30.
Still can't get over that bloke in enquiries.
I remember when I took a train to Retford, I thought
I'd get lost and everything.
Even from Retford you can catch a bus,
and it stops more or less outside the nick.
That was the first time I went by myself
'cos they weren't both at Ranby were they?
No, it were Lincoln. Ranby's women.
I've told him that I'll gladly go and see him
But if he's on about Joe I'm not going
when Jay-Jay's in the nick. 'Cos
with anyone else, yeah, but not his little sister.
I'd love a family reunion. Just my kids, not the steps
That'd be too big. That's the train. Stand up.
When she was born she weighed 8lbs
Jay-Jay was 8lbs, oh come on, was it 8lbs 6?
8lbs 10? Will she talk to me?
I don't know, she's a right snobby cow,
it's her birthday and all today.
She'll know by the name,
it had to go on the form
even if I say I'm Zoe.
Her name's Kathleen Anna Bernadette.

Harp

Tully finally told the tale -
the usual – a castle on a hill,
all the music stolen.
They were thrown out some time later, the heels of words
ringing in the rain.

Lady Looney had long gone,
she mooned about the town,
couldn't hold a tune, they said.
You never knew where you were with her, her frowns,
her penchant for wearing the wrong green gown.

Round and round, seeking her kind,
her face in the running gutters,
the sheen of streets. Many a time,
Roadrunner found her by the fountain,
her breath echoing each thrown stone..

So, the end of the story? She'd stolen a spoon
some said of ivory, others that her white finger
slid from railing to spike as she ran,
pikes, yes, palisades, yes, balconies speak:
notes, round as milk, flew from her eyes.

Verbatim

I'm hiding a gift, one hand behind my back.
Behind us the sky changes, blue, grey, blue grey,
disappearing on the lips like sugar, lightening
above the staggered satellite dishes, transmitters, observation towers.
Now we can see the rain. I wish I were not consoled by this,
I wish I were consoled by ARISE ablaze on the end terrace wall.
I wish I were the busker's fanfare; here I come,
struggling through the entrails of his trombone,
landing upside down, seeing what he sees, the streets, the light.
Oh yes, the gift. I've opened my hand, it's empty.
Take it. If you do, all that's gone before
will never be the same again.

When Pigeons Fall

...and then I sat on the steps of the Council House
between the stone lions who seem
to be guarding something I don't know what
and this is one of my questions;
what are they guarding? Hints of marble,
uniforms, do they not know that I am a king?
That day I asked questions of the air; the pigeons
and these were the questions; when I look at my hand
who am I looking at? When pigeons fall
why don't the cracks stay black, fractured,
yet next day the sky is smooth and blue again?.
The orange flags, stirring above cars in Motor Mart
What country? What song are they singing?
and this drum drum beat beat which says do this do that
every day when I hear it I know I've left my sword somewhere
horse, spurs, glory, words that people heard and answered
all tumbled somewhere by the side of the road.
No-one, not even my Key Worker, who has the answer
to everything in her filing cabinet, can answer these questions.
Why is the fountain triumphant and why can I recognize joy
when I can't remember it ? What do I sound like when I speak
and most of all where among the pigeons is the one
                                        who cries 'you, you'?
When will the doorways pour their light
onto my waiting head?

Remembering Earl

1 small cabbage, 1lb pots, 1pkt.streaky (if cheap)
Rosary at 8. Write to Earl.
The butter sputters in my bent pan
smearing Norah's postcard of the Bridge of Sighs,
which I'd always imagined as puffs of breath,
like broken beads,
barely holding their own.

Our breaths froze in the dark mornings,
as we carried cabbage and bacon to the boys .
That pearl of air was part of me,
but where's it gone? 'You have some fancies' says Norah.
She thinks I'm simple, writing to Death Row
but it's not easy. 'Just be yourself '
the lady from Amnesty said.

During the Sorrowfuls I saw his black finger
tracing my writing on the airmail paper.
During the Joyfuls (which Norah gabbles)
I saw the rare light, like a medal on his breastbone.
During the Glorious Mysteries, his breath rose
from behind the walls like a long-held note
his whole lost body failing to come out.

In The Mandarin

The sound's turned down,
a man reaches for a crying woman,
she flinches as they touch.
Interpreting their lip-sync,
I'd say it's over. Almost.
Now what? No Sesame Toast,
it rarely travels well. Ah, she's here,
a silver orchid behind one ear.
Illuminated beauties compete
behind her head, ivory rice; each grain complete
intimate as pores, bone-white
water-chestnuts. Biting
between each rib, absence tastes
sweet, sour, sweet. I'd wait
for her all night, but the queue
has gone. Her eyes say 'Now, you'

'I'd rather be a ghost at your side
a condemned soul, than be in heaven without you'

The next one chooses BBQ Spare Ribs
with Chilli Sauce, 2 Pepsis, extra chips.
Deftly she folds a napkin, doesn't miss a beat,
the man walks alone down a long street.
Sweet and Sour King Prawns and rice, please
No sound. Perhaps she's Cantonese.

Hymnody

O, voiceless ones without a king
I would not dare to ask you sing
Alleluia! Alleluia!
O, sun and moon deploy your torches
And seek out those who sleep in porches.

O Sister Rage, infect us all
Throw down your cloak of blackest gall
Dolorosa! Dolorosa!
St Francis praised every spore
for fun, his job was learning to be poor

O you who stand in rows in pews
Throw down your hymn-sheets, read the news
Dolorosa, dolorosa!
Or better still, go out and graph
The Devils's work on our behalf.

O Mother City who can't provide
Homes for those who live outside
Dolorosa! Dolorosa!
May your tears turn to hearths and bricks
The cornerstone of politics

Brother Beggar shout out loud
Embarrass all the watching crowd
Dolorosa! Dolorosa!
O Sister Madness share your grief
and take away our unbelief.

Skip

They have lain me deep
in a strata of refuse
Wait. This barge will sail
flood your palisades, your keeps,
'I Return' blazing on the prow.

The Sword in the Stone

I pulled with my strength and the strength of another
drawing on the black and white memory of my mother.

I went on pulling, black blood beating on my ears
remembering the three times I faced my fears

and went to rehab. Strength too came from the time
a stranger shared his last cigarette, the prison pantomime

when Spider played Widow Twankey as tragedy.
Keep pulling; that scout's honour badge was not to be

nor the Army job or even the Pork Pie factory sweep
an alien hand keeps my sword buried deep.

The forms, the cuts, the benefit review
muster with the freezing nights to run me through.

You, great stone, never heard a word I've said, though
I never doubted one day you would turn to bread

Can't go on, but can't stop pulling, and now I am alone.
The sword presses against my heart, the stone is still a stone.

Lost Reel

The script's in that bag there if you don't believe me.
Better still, watch as she jumps on her horse
and veers off into the snow, her black plumed hat
speckled with ice nucleation-active proteins. 'Listen'

I say to my bags, squatting beside me, looking up,
'The tall woman with long feet, walking in the grainy snow
her throaty almost-growl, her fur tippet
could only be my Guenefor, my Jenny. '*Jenny kissed me*

Jenny kissed me, say that health and wealth have missed me'
(reverse tracking shot) the triangular shadows from
					the New York towers
obscure her face. Oh, that such a face should be found
on the ancient spool unwinding as we speak,

through my temporal lobe through to the shot
of empty footprints, already filling up with drifting flakes.
That Garbo played Guinevere, there is no doubt.
The archivists are baffled. They spend their days in museums
while it plays twice nightly, right here, on the street.

Merlin Listens 11

Our Carl lost his job. She said 'Give us a roll-up'
Is this the right bus? Give me the bag.
Anyway, I promised Janey.
If it isn't the 53 we're buggered.
I asked her and she went,
'Well, then you'll be short an' all,
'A roll up'd do nicely.'
What did your Carl do anyway?
After all, a kidney's a kidney.
He was a look-a-like, you know, like the Pope.
He looked like the Pope. Then he died.
He was on the night-bus when he heard,
it was in the paper of the bloke in front.
He said to me 'That's it then. Twenty years'
The fag wasn't the point. She was saying don't give me nothing.
It was all right while it lasted, but he don't look nothing
$\qquad\qquad\qquad\qquad\qquad\qquad$ like the new one.

Round

My moon's pale-ale pearly
says Sir Curly

Bottle's gone walkie-walkie
says Sir Chalky

Shut up about Al Macarooney
says Lady Looney

Shirl's well hot
says Sir Lancelot

Wrong mouth, wrong mouth
says Sir Heading South

Here's to me dear auld Mam
says Sir Ham

If ye knew who she was
says Sir Moz

Shut up the pair of ye
says Sir Hairy McGee

Here's to pay-day
says Sir Kay

Which was fucking yesterday
says Sir Kay

Here's to tomorrow
says Sir Wally Warrow

And my love for him
says Sir Sailor Kim

My heart's love's long gone
says Sir Whisky John

My moon's pale-ale pearly
says Sir Curly

Gallagher's Way

'He has the way of it' said Smudge.
We nodded, drained our glasses,
conjuring Gallagher and his way,
walking everywhere, upturned eyes
seeming sightless (he could see alright)
fixed on something floating above his head.
'A bottle most likely' said Binky,
'or a cup', I said. But we all agreed
that Gallagher has the way of it.

Every day he meets a swan
in the stone lake behind the Museum.
Every day the swan comes. looking
important, like a witness at a line-up,
rearing, in a blink half-snake,
the black line of his face breaking,
Gallagher holding his one piece of bread
over the warning 'Do Not Feed
These swans can be dangerous'.

'He drinks the same way', said Chalky.
'Gazing above the glass for a minute
before raising the next' The way
he buttons his coat precisely,
tied round the middle with a striped necktie,
one hand pressed on his breast pocket
where the bread is, treading steadily,
those upturned eyes unchanging,
never wavering or stumbling

'He'll be in, in a minute', said Smudge,
and we fell quiet, looking at the chair
as if waiting for something to begin.
'Did y'ever see him fall?' asked Percy
'He'll fall down finally,'said Chalky,
when he's had enough, still in his coat'.
'With those eyes, you'd not know the difference'
said Tully, who'd had a few, but Blind Mary
said, 'I'd like a little piece of that bread from him, myself'.

Circumstellar

Surround us, old stars, for the light is indeterminate
wavering according to high tide or spate

lighting the crest of the wave. Our byways
occasionally illuminated, a light thrown slantwise

from a passer-by, a window opens, shuts again
a brief glimpse then, of the silver rain,

yes, our byways, our paths of desire
are lit from above by a cold, invisible fire

or so we tell each other, wandering knights
then one will gesture to the heights

and depths and tell an age-old myth
of permanent suns, fire on warm brick

keys heavy in the hand, the sign 'To Let'
This sun is not unknown to us. It has a name. 'Regret'

Pianola

Yes, I've written in the past on Rizlas,
train timetables, divorce papers, fog,
lines declaring themselves into the deaf air
captured from time to time and immured
in the Museum of the Banned. You won't get in
and I'll never get out. My carrier bags
crouch at my feet, begging the question.
No, I'm too tired for this,
it is all there in black and white, a song of love,
or it would be - it's all been hushed up.

Tonight the pianola plays alone
someone must have sent a message through
from where they call long ago. 'Yes, a double,
if you would be so kind. Now fuck off.' Up to 10 o'clock
I'm a character, later an acronym crackling with anti-social behaviour.
Time to leave. I was just going anyway.
Up the hill where nobody knows, right foot sharp
left foot flat, did you know that I favoured the left?
Did you know that on this very street the Jarrow marchers
sang 'Jerusalem' in thanks for food, then rose up again, silently?

'There Will Be No More Temples in the City'

Based on Ezekiel – Chapters 40-43

At the beginning of the year, on the tenth day of the month, in the twenty-fifth year of our exile.
The length of the rod which the man was holding was six cubits

'Tell us everything you see'

National Grid Gas (defended by steel fence) Pound£leshcontempt appearing, Dovetail Joinery: Exclusive Gold Furniture. Whatever you're planning for in 2012 we can help.

Reckoning by the long cubit which was one cubit and one hand's breadth,

5 star Motors - Car washing incl Sundays, also Parts, Keep Hyson Green Blooming, Jesus4Shariah. Chapatti Junction, Persian Mini-Market, mind the step.

He measured the thickness and height of one wall, each was one rod

Ozi's £ Plus, Demad House Lace Manufacturers, (on a wheelie-bin) 'All the darkness cannot put the light out of a candle' Patik loves Rosie. Kerkuk Restaurant – men only, (on a wheelie-bin) 'Knowledge without Understanding is Empty.'

He measured the threshold of the gateway, each depth was one rod. Each cell was one rod long, and one rod wide, and there was a space of five cubits between the cells

Faith in Action: Enjoy the Fun - Party Games, Please drop your washing off here. Bro, where was ya, I waited 2 hours; Adult Shop. E-**L**-evate School of Motoring, Win your golden ticket here!

Now the cells of the gateway, looking back eastwards, were three in number on each side, all of them same size, and their pilasters on either side were each of the same size

Nutan Jewellers Pawnbrokers-We cash cheques- any cheque considered, The Old General – quiz night most nights, Drongos for Europe tickets here.

He measured the entrance to the gateway; it was ten cubits wide, and the width of the gateway itself was thirteen cubits

Christelle Shop African Hair and Beauty Design. Back in 10. Final Cut – Men's Hair designs, open 'til midnight. Madni Sweet Mart and Pan House, Karczna Pod Zbóbnem.

In front of the cells on each side lay a kerb, one cubit wide; each cell was six cubits by six

Accra Central Market -deals in Ghanaian dishes, Extra Large Jackfruit, Hafiz Iberian Delights. Cost of Botched Police Raids – your Evening Post sold here. Nadia, callers welcome, I am George, a blue-green Macaw with orange shoulders, very worried. Youth for Christ Night Tonight.

The man brought me to the outer court and I saw rooms and a pavement round the court. The pavement ran up to the side of the gateways, as wide as they were long

Skype calls here, Diamond Island - 7p to Ghana. Umani Fashions. Midlands Community Training and Development (boarded–up). Carlton, I love you, if you read this, you'd know.

Gawain's Overcoat

You couldn't call it loud given
the softness of the tweed but somehow
its fibres tugged at you,
like a man in a bar eager to confide.
It was strangely stiff, the kind of coat
which would walk away unaided
leaving its owner shivering and naked
but feeling that his time was up.

'Oxfam' he said, swallowing
his beer. 'It used to be a kilt.'
We settled in the smoke to hear
the story. The last of the line,
the secret burial of the bard;
It might have been. What with the whisky
and the dark eyes of the fella
next to me, I can't remember.

That night he dreamt of walking across
the border, and the coat agitating
around him like a hazel twig
over water, shuddering in tune
with the new winds and the snatched
ouches of crows. The knife-edge
pleats urged him on, perpetually ahead;
the circle of stones.

He was Moses in that coat, seeing
what was before him, but belonging
to the journey behind him. Dressing
in his working clothes (black, dog collar)
he remembered stealing sweets
from Dolly Prosser's and how the old men
competed to spit on the turtle, embossed
on the iron stove in Cappucci's Ices.

One Sunday, old Rowley unexpectedly
spoke in tongues, a worrying thing
for the congregation. Taking communion
to the sick, mountains inflated behind
the terraces, the shine of the cobbles
turned into rivers. He raised his hat
as Mad Sharon folded her thighboots
into a car with no numberplates.

Swedenborg's Drains

On this spot, which you know well
at the bottom of my street,
where it joins the boulevard and the park,
where each year there is a fair,
where tree roots swell
through the paving-stones,
we parted. 'See you next week!'
As we say it, we see it, heads bent
over the table, but I have to go,
the drain men are there
with their rods and cameras.
Next door's cat with exact feet leads
me to the screen they've set up
in my back yard. Inside
an engraved page flutters
open, Emmanuel signals
to William, their effortless angels
stir underground. 'Have a look'
says the drain man. The cat brushes
against blue tunnels, parallel rooms,
where you and I are still
at the bottom of the street,
roots growing from our soles.

The Wedding Horse

Bedecked. Not many horses can say that
of themselves: but I am calm
under red and gold brocade,
the one and only,
stamping gently in the back streets,
my breath rising to the clouds.
Where am I today, earth or Sharam Khand?
8 Brewery St., Nottingham,
waiting for the groom.
Here he comes, held up by five cousins,
patchouli'd cheeks close,
swaying a little. Fair enough,
it's his day, his flash of princedom.
Next week, in his one discount designer suit,
he'll be back in the basement of the call-centre.
It's hell, but he doesn't know it.
Must be off, time to go,
(it's always time to go,
if bliss is your trade).
For I am glorious, I am upward,
gold coat fluttering in the wet pavements
the drainpipes, the roofs.
Simultaneously (not many horses can say that
of themselves) I
'll be outside the Gurdwara Granth Sahib,
43, Pie St, Birmingham.

The Craic

'Joe Mulvaney is a bit of a mixed bag'
observed Colin, once,
the night Joe slid down the barstool quite
slowly and stayed there until closing-time.
A mixed bag; made of stout woven cloth
where workmen used to fold their tools,
indeed there are tools there, some his father's,
betting slips, the forgotten gurgle of Aisling's laughter,
'Let no man write my epitaph' memorised,
a knife, best not to say, a rough bit of his soul broken
off during his last Confession in 1958, his Union card,
the late night drafting for Conor's headstone
Son, ~~Beloved,~~ May Angels Guard Thee, the revving up
of the tractor. Bills. 'Will you have a dance with me?'
the whisper inside a sea-shell, the shine from an unfamiliar
pair of shoes, menacing. The seven times table,
Tower of Ivory, Save us; butter sliding off soda bread.
Well, as Colin said, he was a bit of a mixed bag.
The rest is restoring to itself deep in the peat under Connemara.

You Don't Have to Say Anything

It was probably Spider; but it could have been Gallagher, Woody, Roadrunner, The Weasel, or even Whisky George who told me, about the girl, Jeanie, with pink and black hair held up with silver spikes, who left one day, back very straight and a certain look in her eye.

Now The Weasel or was it Woody fancied Jeanie, although she was rather aloof, never shared her pills or anything. And she saved up and went on the 28a to Blidworth Bottoms and gathered bluebells, armfuls, too many to carry, and people stared at her pink and black hair held up with silver spikes.

Spider said that she'd heard that picking bluebells was illegal so she went to Canning Circus and walked up and down all day in front of the nick, back and forth, back and forth, back and forth, until she was exhausted and an old lady went inside to ask for a cup of water. She was hoping to be arrested just there

because she'd fallen in love with a policeman called Lance. The strangest thing of all was that the nick had been closed for over a year. A few years ago he'd let some buskers off so he'd got the sack and bought an ice-cream van. Woody, who thinks about things, said 'What if she's still there?'

'What do mean, what if she's still there?' 'I mean, in her mind like, walking up and down forever, with her pink and black hair held up with silver spikes, and the bluebells, the blue of the bluebells spilling over like a song while Lance's van played
'Someone to Watch Over Me'

Playing House

The railings ring with Lady Looney's spoons
Growler greets us, crunching like a gravel path,
'Good Afternoon!' I hear an off-key chord among their tunes
could be 'Home Sweet Home'. Step over Spud McGrath
the welcome mat for many a boot,
the front door's grinning in my face. Rat-a-tat-tat!
I've the cheek of a brass knocker. One foot
between step and hall, long dead John takes my hat.
Loss has rusted up the taps, the stairs askew with evil eye.
Gallagher, chimney straight, waiting for vistas to appear,
smoke from his roll-up inscribing on the sky
'We live here'.
Our hopes are walls, a crumbling second skin,
and only the empty ha-ha can stop you breaking in.

Arch

Home for the night, where
I am triumphant over
and above blank stars.
Why do they seek me here, watch
me making a new dead end?

A Merry Christmas to all our Customers

Except Ursula Wilson. Last night
something happened here - was it red wig askew,
glass broken,
or did she, with dreadful look, drain
the crowd of all expectations, like empty pints?

Salt is on the tail of the sluggish gods;
the amazing millennium flower has sprung (roll up!)
strange stars are stirring.
Children look up like winter suns,
they know, but most will lose it

or break it. The grey squirrel thinks he's something;
he doesn't know he's one of seven thousand
and six
city squirrels. He likes it. He doesn't wish
he were giant, or bilingual, or red.

She was a Jezebel, a counter-prophet;
she put grit and stones in souls
as kind and round
as snowballs. The night she slunk into
was a collage of faeces and syringes.

But the ghost of the old cockatoo
(Dead at 117) He knew a thing or two
and found her.
He was wise, had been on the front page
of the Evening Post. He told her something she didn't know,

something I keep forgetting. But
this morning is like parchment unrolling,
lit up, demanding.
For those who are farthest and nearest,
soundless bells are daily ringing.

You asked if I'd seen her. Well,
She'd gathered her rags around her
like a queen,
and was heading for Mansfield. She wavered
at the gallows, but kept on walking.

The Turkey Who Lived on the Hill

For the first time since childhood, I fall asleep
in a city square; digital buzz, neon street cries
murmured questions, half-remembered
invocations call me as I rise, air solid
beneath my flailing hands.
All the cries are all the worlds, Cyrillic, Morse

Braille, Polari. I hear inflections sharper than diamonds,
travelling, foetus-curled, round
and through the chambers of my brain
each one a world, an uninvented tonic sol-fa,
each outstretched appeal, their stories
detailed as a manuscript, saying *love me, love me*;

The two figures on the bridge in the background
of 'The Scream'
The Turkey Who Lived on the Hill.
The triangle player from the Tonga Philharmonia,
'All the Ladies' in Timon of Athens, the other lion in Narnia
Simon of Cyrene.
Myra, selling rewound wool on Upper East Side,
Lysette, who understudied Merle Oberon's body double,
Lowry's Dogs. Lichen on the darkest planet ever found, (TrES-2b),
George, the failed busker, whose only tune was 'Lemon Tree',
the one who wrote in the dust by a wayside shrine,
'Please help Mercedes'

Hitchcock turns a boiled eye as I sink down,
hands brush me, frail as scrolls, crash-landing
into snatched music.

'Like the drip, drip, drip of the raindrops
When the summer shower is through.'

Coolly observing me, Otis The Preacher,
a thousand refractions from his hat's green feather,

'a voice within me keeps repeating 'You, you, you...'

The Order of Brightness

Each Christmas they make an arch of stars
in the precinct, spelling out
'Festive Bonanza – Doug's Used Cars',
but I haven't noticed.

'Do not sit here' warns the arrow,
pointing to the blue-glazed steps – this is the place,
beneath the blank eye of the disappearing sparrow
on the 'Birds of Britain' mural.

My bags look up at me like children
and I begin. I don't need their shreds of paper,
just their fat shapes and rapt attention.
Stars shoot and return.

Wilfrid – cause of death unknown,
James 'Binky' O'Neil - the winter,
Seamus – an infected splinter,
Patsy just decided time to go.
The Weasel, loathed by all, disappeared.
also Feegan with his Assyrian beard,
Whisky John.
Geordie 'The Crow' set on fire
Meredith, climbing St. Aidan's Spire,
Blind Mary, the winter.
Officer, I'm halfway through,
Sir Fingers Donnelly- adieu
Queenie missed her step.

Let go of my arm, I'm done.
You rolling shutters, rattle. Stars
flow down, prick through my overcoat,
your names hurt as I move.

The End

I was taken away by the Queen of Grief
as she glanced from the edge of a fallen leaf.

I was taken away by the Queen of Ire
as I lost my place by the fading fire.

I was taken away by the Queen of Lust
as she kicked like a child in the summer dust.

They steered me through the waters
the sewers , the underground wells
We sailed down the gutters,
the fonts, the saints' cupped hands
to a city on a lake beyond a city
where everyone sleeps on their own soft bed.

Weighed down, these Queens, in their crowns of lead
with all that I have never said.

Biography - Ruth Hobson

Ruth Hobson was born in 1951 in Nottingham where she still lives, works and writes. Her work has been widely published over the years in magazines and journals such as Ambit, Magma, London Magazine, The Delinquent and 'Theology' journal. She has recently been writing song lyrics and two songs 'Angel' and 'Lady Poverty' are on Trillium's latest album 'Kiss My Horse'. As Ruth Shelton, she co-authored 'Making Nothing Happen - Five Poets Explore Faith and Spirituality' Ashgate, 2014.

Palewell Press

Palewell Press is an independent publisher handling poetry, fiction and non-fiction with a focus on books that foster Justice, Equality and Sustainability. The Editor can be reached on enquiries@palewellpress.co.uk

www.ingramcontent.com/pod-product-compliance
Lightning Source LLC
Chambersburg PA
CBHW071322080526
44587CB00018B/3324